# 10 creative ways to make money conveniently

**AUTHOR_JEFFERY BEKEBEN**


ISBN:9798846158450

## DEDICATION

These book is dedicated to all those who ate willing despite the economy of our country to start making money conveniently. These book is highly dedicated to my mom _Nelly Akpoguma who taught me everything I know

# CONTENTS

## ACKNOWLEDGMENTS

Am thankful to Amazon books which help realize my talents am really thankful to them. Secondly i would also like to thank my parents and friends who helped me a lot in finishing this project within the limited time. I am making this project not only to help people but to also increase my knowledge. THANKS AGAIN TO ALL WHO HELPED

# Sell your photos

Effort: Medium

Leverage: Low

Startup costs (out of 5 □): □

Potential earnings: On average, $0.35/image. $0.10–$99.50 per (royalty-free) sale or up to $500 for a photo sold under an extended license.

Modern smartphones have high-quality cameras. The iPhone 13 Pro, for example, has a triple-lens with macro optical zoom capabilities and that can take ultra-wide shots
It's no surprise then that the ever-increasing quality of smartphone cameras has crashed the camera industry. Mid-level cameras were made obsolete when your phone began offering the same quality with 10 times the convenience. You carry your smartphone wherever you go.

But instead of leaving your photos to sit idly in the cloud, you can potentially turn your snapshots into cash—and your smartphone is all the equipment needed to make money on the side while expressing your creative side.

Photographs are like any other product, and in order to successfully sell your photography you need to target an audience of potential customers who want or have a need for them. Start by thinking about the photography style you're most interested in, whether that's landscapes, portraits, or pets.

Then, depending on how you plan to monetize (e.g., by selling prints or offering rights to stock photography sites), see if there's a specific lane or niche you can identify. For example, you may notice that photos of papercraft creations are in demand on stock photography sites but that the current supply is limited. That's a potential opportunity.
The Haute Stock library was born out of this concept. Its founder, Rachel Rouhana, was "frustrated with the lack of stylish stock photography available for women business owners." So she created Haute Stock to fill that gap in the market.

Learn more: How to Sell Photos Online (For Both Amateur and Pro Photographers)

Once you've found your niche, start building a following on visual-heavy platforms like Instagram or Pinterest. Snap some niche-specific photos, use a free photo editor to polish them up, then sell them on sites like Adobe Stock, Shutterstock, and TourPhotos.

Monitor which style works best through the platform's analytics. Pinterest, for example, shows how many link clicks a photograph has had. Are there any similarities between your top-performing photographs?

Use your social media accounts to tease your paid content—bloggers and business owners always need stock photos. You could pitch directly to your target business owner, asking whether they'd be willing to pay for your photos—and how much they're willing to pay. For example: you might identify the audience for your pet-related photos as dog retailers who are willing to pay $25 per stock photo.

Bear in mind that you'll need to price your stock photos on three factors: the demand for photos in that industry, the price competitors are charging, and the fees you're paying to take the photos themselves. If you're shooting people, you'll need to pay them, and if you're shooting locations you'll usually need permission or to pay a fee. Build this into your pricing to make sure you're not losing more money than you're making.

By selling your images through one of these platforms, you could turn your hobby into your first $100 on the side

## Print on demand

Effort: Low

Leverage: High

Startup costs: □□

Potential earnings: Depends on the products you sell. The average t-shirt has a profit margin between $5 and $8.

Print on demand is a low-risk way to make money that, unlike traditional dropshipping, lets you leverage your creative talents. Here's how it works: You work with a supplier to customize (or white label) products such as books, t-shirts, phone cases, or other merchandise. You add your design to a plain item, then the supplier prints and delivers your products to customers on a per-order basis so you don't have to hold inventory in order to start selling

Since you can take the lion's share of logistics and operations work off your plate, thanks to Shopify apps like Printful, Lulu Direct, and Printify, you'll have more time to focus on design, branding, and marketing your products. It's a very accessible business model if you're working a full-time job. You can get creative with your own talents or commission a freelance designer to help you with patterns or full-blown product designs.

Since your customized products will be manufactured once a customer places an order, you also won't have to pay for the items until you've sold them.

Print on demand is a superb model for creatives who want to get involved with their products but don't have time to commit to making or manufacturing them. It combines the ability to be expressive and to build a distinct brand with the ease of dropshipping, making it a nice sandbox to start your side hustle in.

"Free Webinar:"
Go on online to register

How to quickly start a profitable print-on-demand store"

## Teach online classes

Effort: High

Leverage: Medium

Startup costs: □□□

Potential earnings: Beginners can make between $10 and $20 per hour. More experienced or niche class teachers charge upward of $3,000 per course.

Turning your industry knowledge into an online course is a smart way to make extra money—even as a complement to an existing product-based business. Take Babbel for Business and Sugarlash Pro Academy. Both online courses have a niche customer base yet still bring in extra money for the course creators.

The creators behind Sugarlash Pro Academy found a unique niche they were knowledgeable about and created a series of profitable online courses around the topic.

You can start making money by teaching classes in an area you're interested in. What can you talk about for hours on end? What do your family and friends ask for your advice on? The answers are likely a great class idea. But remember, a huge part of any online course's success is the audience who purchases it.

Some niches might not be as profitable as others, so check whether there's high demand for your course topic before investing time in creating it. Generally speaking, you want to look for audiences willing to pay money in order to make progress. Passionate hobbyists or professionals who are willing to invest in their craft are prime examples

Next, plan the flow of your course. Think about the topics you want to cover and create content for each section. This could be a one-off lesson sold as a class or a curriculum of content on a similar theme offered as a course.

You can host and distribute your content on platforms like Shopify, Udemy, Teachable, SkillShare, or LinkedIn Learning, all of which allow creators to monetize their course. This offers an added bonus versus selling a course through your own site by giving you a built-in distribution tool.

Sure, you'll need to spend some time promoting your course. But once you've invested time in creating the content, your investment is basically done. The time and money you spend developing the course is upfront, meaning you'll only need to fork out marginal costs if and when you update it.

## Recommend your favorite products

Effort: Low

Leverage: Medium

Startup costs: □

Potential earnings: Unlimited.

Chances are, you've got a list of products you couldn't live without. You refer one of those products to your friend, and they soon feel the same. Affiliate marketing is a way to monetize your passion for helping people connect with the right product.

The affiliate marketing model works by recommending products to your network and receiving a bonus—usually a percentage of the sale price in commission or gift cards—as a reward. Most companies, including Amazon, Uber, and eBay, offer a refer-a-friend incentive.

You could take things a step further by recommending your favorite products to a bigger audience through blogging or posting on social media. Wirecutter has a team of staff writers who create product-centric content for its audience. The site monetizes through the commissions they receive for referrals.

This is how most influencers and bloggers make money online aside from offering sponsored posts. Wirecutter and BuzzFeed, to look at two examples, both employ staff writers and freelance contributors to write review-focused content that's monetized with affiliate links. Affiliates receive a commission when their audience purchases based on their recommendation.

These reviews aren't spammy—there's no pushy feeling that forces you into making a purchase just because the influencers will receive a commission. Their reviews are in-depth, unbiased, and genuinely make it easier for you to find the right product.

That's the basic idea of great affiliate marketing: providing additional education and context that can be challenging for the official company to present in a genuine way. Affiliate content is formed around unbiased options, simply referring products you enjoy.

It's relatively easy to get started with affiliate marketing—particularly if you're an existing customer of a brand. Search the brand's website and see if it offers a refer-a-friend program. (If it doesn't, you can always email to enquire.) Ask friends to use your link or code when they purchase from that brand and you'll both get a reward.

## Rent your unused space

Effort: Low

Leverage: Medium

Startup costs: 

Potential earnings: $300–$3,000/year.

Statista reports that the rent price per square foot of storage space has steadily risen the last few years. Extra space has become more valuable. So if you have some extra space in your home, you might be able to make some money renting it out.

One example is your backyard. You can treat it as a side-hustle opportunity by listing it on camping websites or Airbnb and charging people to pitch their tent there. Create boundaries with the people you open your camping space to—such as whether they're allowed to use your indoor toilet, access your home, or light barbecues on your grass.

You might also want to consider limiting your space to a specific group of people, like families or those with young children. Even if you charge just for the pitch space, it's a superb option for making your first $100 on the side.

You also can partner with Rent the Backyard. It'll build a small apartment in your yard for free and split the profits with you when you rent it out. The company's website says a homeowner in San Francisco could make up to $12,000 in their first year. But bear in mind that this is a big commitment in return for the large paycheck.

Similarly, for a small monthly fee you could rent the parking space that comes with your home or apartment to family, friends, or one of the many drivers who spend 17 hours per year looking for a parking spot—a huge source of frustration for commuters. This is an especially great side-hustle idea if you use the car space but aren't at home during the day.

The amount you'll earn depends on where your parking space is. New York, for example, has an average monthly parking cost of $600, but people in downtown Austin pay just $219 per month.

You can use sites like Parkopedia or Craigslist to check out your competition. Find what people in your location are charging for their parking space, then price your spot competitively. Pop into local offices and ask whether any staff would be interested in renting your spot

## . Sell your services

Effort: High

Leverage: Low

Startup costs: □

Potential earnings: $20+ per hour.

The gig economy is on the rise. An increasing number of people are performing work as independent contractors or freelancers who work for other organizations on a flexible or temporary basis to earn money online

Freelancing or service-based businesses are the second-most popular side hustle. In fact, Upwork's 2021 Freelance Forward survey reported that 59 million Amercians performed freelance work in 2021.

You can get involved by selling your services. Think about what you're good at or want to learn. There's probably a company looking to employ someone like you on a project basis, as opposed to a full-time contract.

Once you've found your special skill, start getting experience on sites like Upwork, TaskRabbit, or Fiverr. Be wary that other freelancers, especially those who don't know how to position their services, might charge pennies for similar work, and that there's a risk of pricing way too low to beat them in the battle for clients. A great place to start is the average hourly rates in your country for a specific profession. The average hourly rate for a marketer in the US, for example, is $33.

Decide what services you could offer by looking at the skills you've nailed in your day job:

Are you praised for the way you organize your email inbox? You could make a great virtual assistant.
Do you communicate with co-workers and summarize your meeting minutes for your team? The leap to writing isn't too far.
Can you listen to a client and deliver exactly what they want? You could offer party planning services for people in your area

You could also take a look at the tasks you enjoy doing or those you'd like to develop. Let's say you're working in a marketing agency as your full-time job. You enjoy social media posting but don't enjoy advertising. You could reach out to clients who only want social media content and offer that as your standalone service. Just make sure there isn't a non-compete clause in your full-time contract. (It's worth chatting with your boss to double check.)

You'll also need to decide on a schedule for your side gig. Some companies hire remote staff that don't need to be present in the office. Look for that type of role if you'd prefer the flexibility that comes with remote-friendly work. Similarly, if you thrive being around other people or find that kind of work isolating (even on the side), offer to join other companies in their office when you're free. You'll do the same work—just in their office

You might need to spend a while creating your portfolio—a collection of work that proves you're good at the service you're selling—before you can demand higher rates.

However, you can start with lower rates and potentially use your service offering as a springboard to starting your own business. First, see whether there's a demand for your service, whether you can fit the work into your schedule, and how much clients are willing to pay you. You might find a hidden home business opportunity to make this income stream your main one.

Service-based side hustles are high margin, and can be very profitable and quick to pay off. But the downside is they're usually a bit harder to scale into an asset that can run without you. You are your business—you'll need to be on-hand to do the work, or at least oversee it if you grow to the point where you're able to subcontract work to another freelancer and maximize profit.

## Test websites

Effort: Low

Leverage: Low

Startup costs: □

Potential earnings: $10 per test on average.

You form an impression of a website when you visit it, and companies are always looking for feedback on their site. So you could get paid for sharing your thoughts, whether it's on design, content, or usability.

This is a great side hustle for people who have spare time at an office—maybe on their lunch break. Sites like UserTesting pay $10 per 20-minute test, which might not sound like much, but if you do one every lunch break for two weeks, these small tasks will have earned you your first $100 on the side.

Similarly, you can volunteer to take part in focus groups. Designers, copywriters, and marketers are always looking for feedback on their new campaign. You could email them and volunteer your time to help, asking for a small incentive—like a cash reward or gift card—in return for your time and opinion.

## Sell your art

Effort: High

Leverage: High

Startup costs: □□□

Potential earnings: $20–$20,000/month.

If you're a budding artist, selling your work is a great side hustle idea

It's a simple way to make money from your hobby—especially when you combine it with the print-on-demand model. Transfer your illustrations onto a physical product (like a t-shirt or coffee mug) and create an online store for your items. You'll only pay the fee for the item once you sell the product.

Or you could create an online library of your artwork. Work on building a following, then offer quick, personalized art in return for a small fee. This is a great way for budding artists to work on their craft, making extra money on the side and building an audience as they grow. Sites like Buy Me A Coffee let people donate the cost of a coffee in return for your custom work.

Talented artists can combine their art with a service and offer made-to-order illustrations. Both businesses and the general public often look for custom illustrations through sites like Etsy or Fiverr.

Alternatively, you can use Shopify to sell your art directly to customers. You're able to print several copies of your work and sell them through your own online shop. This means you can set your own pricing, manage your inventory, and have full control over your illustrations

# Sell your stuff online

Effort: Low

Leverage: Low

Startup costs: □

Potential earnings: Anywhere from $1–$1,000+.

Chances are, you have stuff you aren't using and it's taking up space. In fact, Statista reported that only 8.3% of all US self storage units were vacant in 2020, with that number projected to continue to decline through 2024. We all have stuff we don't need and could probably sell for good money.

After you go through your things and find all the stuff you want to sell, all you have to do is take a good picture, post it on a site that will get it seen, and write a good description. No longer do you have to suffer through a painful garage sale—you can do everything online.

You can use larger marketplaces like eBay and Facebook Marketplace to get your stuff seen or you can use something that caters to the specific things you're selling. Like Chairish, which is geared toward home decor and furniture, or RubyLane, which focuses on vintage and antique items

The best part about selling your stuff is you get to declutter your home or office and it doesn't cost you a thing to start selling—just your time.

"Learn More: 20 Online Selling Sites and Marketplaces to Sell Your Stuff".

# Do random tasks

Effort: Low

Leverage: Low

Startup costs: □

Potential earnings: Average of $35/hr, but depends on task and experience.

The Pew Research Center reports that in 2021, 16% of Americans earned money through an online gig platform. Getting paid to do random tasks for others is a legit side hustle and a great way for people to make money fast.

There are many apps where you can sign up to offer simple services like moving furniture and helping to mount a TV on a wall. If you have a skill, that's great, but a lot of these tasks just require someone who has some extra time.

The best part is, you set your own schedule and rates. You can keep this as a side hustle or turn it into a full-blown online business. You're in complete control of how much you want to work and how much you want to make.

Below is a shortlist of several apps where you can sign up to be a handyman or random task contractor.

TaskRabbit: a general app that offers everything from home deliveries to gardening.
Handy: similar to TaskRabbit, but also offers plumbing and electrical work.
Fancy Hands: offers assistants of any type to its customers, whether it's picking up dry cleaning or walking the dog.
Thumbtack: helps find local pros like wedding DJs or photographers.
Staffy: finds temps for employers in essentially any industry, oftentimes on short notice or same day.

## Give your opinion on online surveys

Effort: Low

Leverage: Low

Startup costs: □

Potential earnings: On average about $1 per survey.

Signing up with online survey sites is a great way to pad your pocket with a few extra bucks. Just apply to the survey site of your choice and put in your interests and survey preferences. Then you get to choose which surveys you want to fill out.

You don't need any specialized knowledge or expertise. These companies are just looking for people willing to take the time to answer their questions thoroughly.

Some online surveys will take five minutes and others might take you over an hour. You can decide what sort of commitment you want to make and what survey rate is right for you

There are many companies and survey sites looking for your opinion, but here's a shortlist to get you started.

One Opinion
Survey Junkie
Opinion Outpost
MyPoints
Swagbucks

## Become an online juror

Effort: Medium

Leverage: Low

Startup costs: □

Potential earnings: Usually $5–$10 per case.

According to the USFinancial Education Foundation, there are over 40 million lawsuits filed each year and more than one million registered lawyers. These lawyers sometimes need to practice presenting their case to real people. That's where you come in.

## Organize other people's things

Effort: Medium

Leverage: Low

Startup costs: □

Potential earnings: $30–$130/hr.

If Marie Kondo has taught us anything, it's that sometimes, all we need is a little help organizing the things in our lives. If you're someone who has a knack for organization and likes to help people, this might be the side gig of your dreams.

On average, a professional organizer makes about $50 per hour in the US. This can involve more than just putting a bunch of stuff in boxes. It means understanding your clients and finding an organizational system that works for them and their lives.

Professional organizers are hired for more than organizing items in a house. You can also help with restructuring a business, digital information organization, time management, and even feng shui

You can sign up on contractor sites like Thumbtack and Westtenth. From there, you can specify what your skills are and your rates. Then get to organizing!

## Become a translator

Effort: Low

Leverage: Low

Startup costs: □

Potential earnings: Anywhere from $10–$100/hr.

In 2021, 46.2 million immigrants entered the US. The world is becoming more and more connected, so if you're fluent in more than one language, you can use that to make some extra money.

With sites like Translate.com, Unbabel, and even Fiverr, it's easy to find gigs asking for translation services. Some sites require you to take a test to show your fluency level and then base your pay rate off it.

There are sites that specialize in blog posts and proofreading, and sites that only do mobile apps or web comics. If there are words involved, you'll most likely find a translation gig as well.

Here's a shortlist of 5 sites to get you started:

•Tethras: work with mobile app developers.
•TextMaster: web content, writing, and proofreading.
•American High-Tech Transcription and •Reporting: provides services to law enforcement and government agencies.
•Aberdeen Languages Services: business translation services.
•GlobaLink Translations: specializes in health care, pharmaceutical, psychological, and research translations

If you have specialized knowledge in another language, that's a whole other avenue you can delve into. For example, under the Affordable Care Act Section 1557, all hospitals are required to offer competent translators for their patients. And because you'd be offering a specialized type of translation, you can charge more per hour for your services.

The great thing about this gig is you can make your own hours and set your own rates. You also can help people who otherwise would feel lost in legal or medical situations. On top of that, if learning languages is something you enjoy, you can get paid to continue your studies.

# Become a mystery shopper

Effort: Low

Leverage: Low

Startup costs: □

Potential earnings: Average $20/hr.

If you like shopping, why not get paid to do it? Mystery shoppers are hired to report about their experiences in specific stores. They're usually called in when a complaint or concern has been raised about that store.

Because of that, your duties can include anything from taking pictures of the storefront to buying a specific item and recording your shopping experience from start to finish. How much you get paid for each job is going to depend on what it is you're asked to do.

While this gig won't replace your day job, you can make some extra cash while you're out and about. With sites like Bestmark and IntelliShop, it's easy to find the mystery shopper gig right for you.

But be careful, there are mystery shopper scams out there. You should never have to pay to become a mystery shopper. Also, keep in mind, many times your travel costs are not included, so factor that into the jobs you accept.

# ABOUT THE AUTHOR

JEFFERY BEKEBEN, born in 1999 was brought up in Nigeria. Made his first $100 at the age of 18 through figuring out the convenient ways of making money. His a graphic designer and uses it to earn money

www.ingramcontent.com/pod-product-compliance
Lightning Source LLC
LaVergne TN
LVHW010514160826
845677LV00012B/2854

* 9 7 9 8 8 4 6 1 5 8 4 5 0 *